Contents

KU-729-369

Introduction

For many millions of people in Europe and East and Southeast Asia, World War II introduced the experience of living under the control of a foreign power, and often a military government.

At the start of the war in Europe, Germany's tactic of Blitzkrieg, or 'lightning war', brought rapid victories over Poland, Belgium, the Netherlands and northern France, followed by parts of Scandinavia and the Balkans. The Germans imposed military government, but they largely left civilian populations to continue with their daily lives, although they introduced regulations to restrict their freedoms.

From the middle of 1941, German forces also brought large areas of Soviet territory under their control. This was a different form of occupation. It was part of Adolf Hitler's policy of *Lebensraum* ('living room'). The policy aimed to seize land for German expansion – which left no room for the peoples already living there. They were forced out or murdered in large numbers. The chief victims of this policy were Europe's Jews, who were earmarked for extermination in the Holocaust, but other groups also suffered great losses.

Japan and Asia

In Asia, meanwhile, the Japanese presented their territorial expansion as an anti-colonial movement to rid the region of European and American rule. While some Asians welcomed the change, many found the Japanese as unwelcome as their previous colonial rulers. The Japanese were mainly interested in resources, and treated conquered peoples harshly.

Resistance and Refugees

In both Europe and Asia, people resisted occupation to various degrees. For most people resistance took the form of small gestures of defiance as they continued with their daily lives. But thousands of people risked their lives by carrying on active resistance, spying for the Allies, assassinating collaborators and sabotaging roads and railways.

Throughout the war, people made homeless by the conflict sought new places to live. In the aftermath of the conflict, Germans from 'Greater Germany' joined the millions who faced a future of uncertainty and aggression at the hands of their former neighbours. As the clear-up after the war began, some 40 million people were trying to get home or to find a new home. Jews, Germans and citizens of the Soviet Union dominated one of the greatest movements of population the world has ever seen.

⇒ **German soldiers in Paris hold a victory parade at the Arc de Triomphe in June 1940. The Germans occupied half of France and set up a 'puppet' government in the other part, called Vichy France.**

Occupied Peoples

QUISLING

Vidkun Quisling was a nationalist politician in Norway who after the German invasion in 1940 was appointed by the Nazis as minister-president of the Norwegian government. He governed as a Nazi 'puppet' for the rest of the war. After the defeat of Germany he was tried as a traitor and executed. Today the word 'quisling' is still used to mean a traitor.

⇑ Vidkun Quisling (right) welcomes a visiting German officer to Norway. Quisling encouraged Norwegians to join the SS and helped the Nazis deport Jews to the death camps.

German and Japanese conquests created vast empires in Europe and Southeast Asia by the end of 1942. Life for those living under their rule changed overnight.

Millions of people found themselves under Axis occupation. German control covered France, Belgium, the Netherlands, Luxembourg, Poland, Denmark, Norway, Finland, the Baltic States – Estonia, Latvia and Lithuania – Yugoslavia, Greece, part of Russia, Ukraine, northern Italy and parts of North Africa. Japan, meanwhile, ruled Malaya, Hong Kong, the Philippines, Indonesia (then known as the Dutch East Indies), Singapore, French Indochina – part of modern Vietnam – Burma and parts of China.

Means of Government

The experience of Axis rule varied in different countries. The Nazis governed countries in three ways. They might be governed directly from Berlin, under the control of a Reich governor; they might be placed under a civil administration that followed German policies and laws; or they might be occupied by the German Army.

⇒ **With the Eiffel Tower in the background, Adolf Hitler (front, second from right) and other senior Nazi officials tour Paris in July 1940, after the German occupation of the French capital.**

REICH GOVERNOR

A Reich governor was a senior Nazi who was appointed by the government in Berlin to run an occupied territory. In everyday matters, governors had some personal freedom, but ultimately they obeyed the will of Adolf Hitler.

Denmark, for example, kept its elected government and its monarchy, although it was tightly controlled by the German foreign office. Northern and western France were occupied by the military, while the Netherlands became what was in effect a German province, governed by the Netherlands Reich Commission. In all cases, however, Axis rule had certain similarities. It was heavily centralised, with states being run from Berlin and Tokyo, respectively. It was strict and repressive. Forms of self-expression and

COLLABORATORS

Many people in occupied countries tried to get along with the occupiers, simply because it made daily life easier. Some actively helped the occupiers, such as by reporting possible resistance to the occupation. Some women had relationships with individual occupation soldiers, or even had their children. After the war, many collaborators were punished by their own countrymen. French women with German boyfriends, for example, were stripped in public and had their heads shaved.

the media were tightly controlled by the invaders; protest or displays of nationalism were entirely crushed. Punishments were often harsh and brutal.

Most populations were issued with official identity papers that had to be carried at all times. Failure to do so could result in imprisonment or even execution: the same fate awaited anyone who broke the nightly curfew and was found on the street after dark.

The harshest occupation in Europe was in the east. There, and in southern Europe, military government was normal. Ostland (East Land) included eastern Poland, the Baltic states and Belarus. Central Poland was known as the General Government. Western Poland simply became part of Germany. Further east, in territory captured from Russia and Ukraine, the Germany army shared government with the feared SS.

⇐ **This poster advertises a book about Pierre Laval, who in 1942 became head of government in Vichy France. Laval believed that collaborating with the Germans offered the best hope for France. He was executed for treason after the war.**

The Gestapo

The means of control was the Gestapo, the political police of the German Reich Security Main Office, established in 1934 by Heinrich Himmler. It was responsible for preventing perceived threats to the German state or the Nazi Party. At its height, the Gestapo employed 30,000 agents and a whole network of informers who reported on suspected political criminals both inside Germany and throughout the occupied territories.

It took very little to be viewed as a political criminal – anyone could fall under suspicion. There was no system of courts or trials. The Gestapo had the power to issue orders – 'orders of protective custody' – which gave them the right to imprison anyone without trial and without any time limit. Many of those who were seized were never seen again. They were simply executed while in Gestapo custody.

⇒ Allied propaganda like this poster highlighted the brutality of the Nazis' treatment of occupied peoples.

NAZI RIPS AMERICAN FLAG IN A. BROTMAN'S POSTER

This is the Enemy

❝We have given most of Europe to Hitler. Let us try to hold on to what we have left.❞

PIERRE LAVAL, LEADER OF VICHY FRANCE

DEATH SQUADS

The Einsatzgruppen of the SS were mobile death squads who were responsible for rounding up and killing about a million Jews and others in eastern Europe. Arriving in a village, they herded their victims together and forced them to strip naked. Then they shot them at the edge of the trenches where they buried the bodies. Death squads operated throughout what are now Poland, Ukraine, the Baltic States and Russia. At Babi Yar in Ukraine, they killed more than 33,000 Jews in two days in 1941.

⇑ Stripped naked, Jewish women and their children stand by a pit in eastern Europe shortly before their murder by Einsatzgruppen. Local people often helped the Germans round up their victims.

Death Squads

Both the Germans and the Japanese believed that they were racially superior to other peoples – and it was those peoples they judged inferior who suffered most under their occupation. In Japan, that included the Chinese and other southeast Asians (see page 13). In Nazi propaganda, the Poles, Russians and Baltic Europeans were subhuman. They had no right even to live.

In eastern Europe SS death squads – the Einsatzgruppen – killed millions of civilians, especially Jews and those considered to be intellectuals. In Poland 2.5 million Jews were either murdered or sent to concentration camps. In occupied Russia the Einsatzgruppen murdered about 3 million civilians, about half of whom were Jews. Regular German soldiers were also reponsible for causing many deaths, particularly by taking food and leaving villagers to starve to death.

Reprisals

The Germans used mass execution as a form of reprisal to any attack on German soldiers. In Russia, the death of a single German might lead to the destruction of a whole village and the murder of its inhabitants. In the west, German reprisals were also out of all proportion to the attacks that inspired them. When Italian partisans ambushed German troops in

Eyewitness
BRIAN READ

Brian Read was a schoolboy on Jersey when the Germans occupied the Channel Islands in July 1940.

'Many people were frightened that their house would be attacked if it did not show a white flag. My mother hung a sheet out of the window.'

DAILY LIFE IN PARIS

After the Germans occupied Paris in May 1940, Parisians faced frequent shortages of food and other basics. The best goods, including coffee, were reserved for the Germans. The electricity supply was often interrupted, especially later in the war. However, the cinema and the opera remained popular among Parisians and occupiers, alike. French women used various ways to maintain the stylish appearance for which they were renowned, recycling old clothes and making their own shoes.

⇐ **German soldiers salute officers enjoying a sidewalk café in Paris on 14 July, 1940 – Bastille Day, France's first national day under German occupation.**

March 1944, the Germans killed 335 civilians in caves near Rome; in France, 642 villagers of Oradour-sur-Glane were killed by an SS company because Maquis (French resistance) were active in the area. The villagers were herded into barns and a church, which were then set on fire. Anyone who tried to run from the buildings was machine-gunned down.

Everyday Occupation

Even for those who escaped the harshest forms of repression, German control

CHANNEL ISLANDS

The Channel Islands – Guernsey, Jersey and some smaller islands – were the only part of Britain to be occupied by the Germans. The British decided not to defend the islands, which had no strategic value, and the Germans landed in June 1940. During the war the local government practiced a policy of 'passive cooperation'. There was no organised resistance, but individual islanders made anti-German gestures such as painting 'V' for 'victory' in public places and listening to BBC broadcasts.

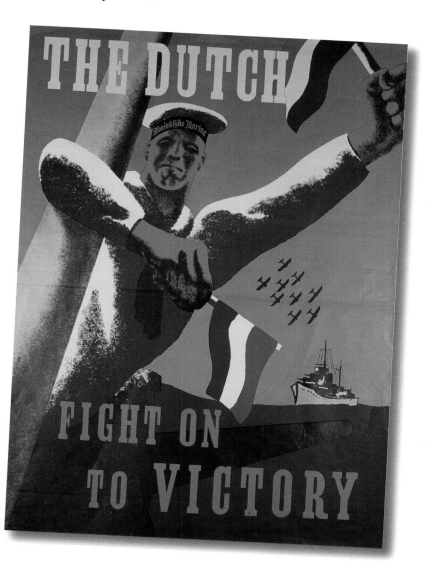

THE DUTCH

FIGHT ON TO VICTORY

brought great hardship. The Germans taxed the occupied countries for the cost of occupation, taking national resources such as food. While the Danes struggled to find enough to eat, for example, the Germans took enough farm produce from Denmark to feed 8 million people. Farm produce and natural resources such as coal had to be sold to German businesses at as little as half the market price.

Meanwhile, the Germans simply took the best goods and food for themselves, leaving the native population with very little. German soldiers in France, for example, confiscated so much coffee that the French had to resort to making coffee from acorns. No petrol or tyres were available for nonmilitary use, so driving virtually ceased.

⇐ **This poster was intended to remind the American public that the peoples of occupied countries, such as the Netherlands, continued the fight against the Germans, either by serving in other armed forces or by joining resistance movements.**

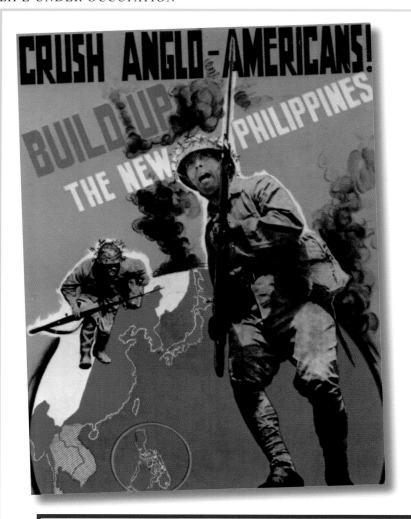

⇐ The Japanese appealed to the Filipinos to join an anti-imperialist cause, but had little success in recruiting supporters from among the populations of occupied countries.

Japanese Occupation

The Japanese believed that they had to acquire an empire in Asia in order to provide the raw materials they needed for their small, crowded home islands.

In particular they wanted access to sources of food and oil. They disguised their real aims, however, by proclaiming the Greater East Asia Co-Prosperity Sphere. The Japanese promised their neighbours that they would create an Asia ruled by Asians, from which the Europeans and Americans had been expelled. When the western imperialists had been removed, the Asian countries would be allowed self-rule.

The reality was very different. A few countries were indeed allowed to keep

JAPANESE OCCUPATION

The Japanese army enforced strict discipline on the peoples it governed. The Japanese had been taught that they were superior to other races, and that anyone who surrendered rather than being killed deserved no respect. That meant that they treated the Chinese and other Asians cruelly, as they were inferior peoples.

⇒ Aided by a Chinese policeman (right), Japanese soldiers with bayonets guard a street in Tientsin, China, in 1939. Civilians could be executed for failing to salute a Japanese soldier.

⇑ **A memorial marks the site of the Manzanar relocation camp in the California desert. The U.S. policy of interning Japanese citizens has been widely criticised since the war.**

INTERNMENT

Many minority groups found themselves in enemy territory at the start of the war. Large numbers of British citizens in Hong Kong, Singapore and China fell under Japanese control, for example. Such 'enemy aliens' were usually held in internment camps for the duration of the conflict, often in harsh conditions. In the United States, meanwhile, Japanese–Americans were moved from coastal regions to 'relocation camps' in the middle of the country, where there was less chance of them helping any Japanese invasion. This was a different kind of internment because the inmates were usually U.S. citizens. Indeed, some young men from the camps volunteered for the army, even though their families were detained.

their own governments, including Burma and French Indochina. French Indochina, now part of Vietnam, was governed by a government on behalf of the collaborationist Vichy regime, which governed France according to Nazi policies.

Thailand was actually rewarded for supporting the Japanese with territory taken from Malaya and Burma. Japanese military governments took over in Hong Kong and Singapore, Borneo, New Guinea and the Dutch East Indies (now Indonesia). But there was no sign of the promised self-rule, although in Malaya the military government promised there would be self-rule in the future.

Japan in China

In China, the Japanese had occupied Manchuria since 1931 and much of the rest of the country by 1937. The Japanese occupiers had been responsible for many atrocities against the Chinese population, including the so-called Rape of Nanking in 1937, in which they had murdered up to half of the 600,000 inhabitants of the former Chinese capital. Japanese troops had used live Chinese for bayonet practice and held competitions to see who could behead most Chinese prisoners in a particular time period. Meanwhile, the Japanese were constantly taking natural resources from their Chinese territories.

All Chinese had to wear identity badges and, like all people in captured territories, had to bow to any Japanese soldier who passed them. A failure to bow could be punished with a beating or even death. Partisan operations against the Japanese were met with the 'three alls' – 'kill all, burn all, loot all'. Japanese units would target a village, massacre its inhabitants, take everything of value and burn down the buildings.

Meanwhile, the quantities of resources that the Japanese removed – 22 million barrels of oil a year, for example – left the native populations facing poverty; the Japanese seized so much rice that starvation became common among conquered peoples. Still governments maintained the sham of supporting the Greater East Asia Co-Prosperity Sphere, but without the support of their citizens.

Eyewitness
PAMELA DE NEUMANN

Australian nurse Pamela de Neumann was interned by the Japanese after the fall of Singapore.
'The Japanese starved us and we had to scrounge what we could from the jungle and we also boiled banana skins. All the prisoners eventually contracted beriberi and fever and many thousands died. I slept on a concrete slab and dug roads, latrines and graves for three and a half years.'

⇓ **Filipino boys stand in front of a list of rules for how to treat occupying troops, such as 'Salute to the Japanese soldiers when you meet them.'**

Welcome Occupation

There were some countries in which occupation was welcomed. In Asia, the Burmese did indeed see the Japanese as their liberators from British rule. The Burmese Independence Army who formed the goverment, however, treated the native Burmese very harshly. In India, the Bengali politician Subhas Chandra Bose formed the Indian National Army from Indian prisoners captured by the Japanese; eventually he led a force of 20,000. Bose believed that fighting with the Japanese was the best way to free India from British rule.

In Europe, meanwhile, many Ukrainians welcomed the arrival of the Nazis. They had suffered under Joseph Stalin's totalitarian communist regime in the 1930s. Some 1.2 million volunteered to work as labourers for the German forces. Meanwhile, in virtually all occupied countries the Germans were able to persuade eager recruits to join the ranks of the

<== German soldiers in Bologna, northern Italy. Germany occupied the region after Italy's surrender to the Allies in September 1943 and set up a puppet republic under former dictator Benito Mussolini.

overseas units of the Waffen SS. To some young Europeans, Hitler's vision of a militarised, racially pure, highly disciplined society was attractive enough to fight for.

'Doing the Least Harm'

Even when people did not welcome occupation, many civilians effectively collaborated with the occupiers. The scale of collaboration varied widely, however. In many countries, businessmen and others had to get along with the occupiers in order to continue making a living. The Belgians, for example, called this kind of daily collaboration 'the policy of doing the least harm'.

In other places, politicians and local officials actively helped the occupying forces. In Vichy France Pierre Laval's government assisted the Germans in the deportation of French Jews to extermination camps. Collaborationist governments also came to power in Norway, where the administration of Vidkun Quisling followed fascist policies. In Greece, a military government took power. In Croatia, meanwhile, the government of Ante Paveliae declared itself independent from Yugoslavia and began rounding up and killing Jews and Serbs.

CROATIA

The Croatian decision to help the Nazis reflected a long history of tension with the neighbouring Serbs. Continuing Serb resentment of Croat collaboration with the Nazis was partly blamed for the wars that broke out in former Yugoslavia in 1991 and continued until 1995.

Forced Labour

In Europe, Germany developed a large-scale plan to exploit workers in occupied territory. The German economy depended on this plan in order to maintain the war effort.

Germany depended on foreign workers. Its population was relatively small compared to that of the combined Allies, and many of its men had been conscripted into the armed services. German economists had long recognised that the country would not be able to maintain a war economy unless it recruited additional manpower as forced labour from occupied countries.

Some foreign workers volunteered to go to Germany, usually to escape poverty and unemployment. About 400,000 volunteers from Belgium moved to Germany, along with nearly 250,000 Poles. In all, Germany was home to some two million volunteer workers from the occupied countries by August 1941.

⇒ **This poster recruited Norwegians for an SS 'skihunter' battalion. Norwegian leader Vidkun Quisling encouraged recruits to join the German forces.**

WORK CAMPS

Foreign workers who were forcibly moved to Germany or other parts of its empire were usually housed in purpose-built camps. These were crowded barrack-like huts with minimal comforts and poor food supplies. The camps were enclosed by fences or barbed wire and guarded to make sure that the workers could not leave the camp. In effect they were prisoners, and they were subject to harsh discipline intended to keep them working as hard as possible – in some cases literally until they had worked themselves to death.

⇒ **Prisoners haul a heavy load in Dachau, the first Nazi work camp. Dachau was set up in 1933, shortly after the Nazis came to power, and provided a pool of slave labour.**

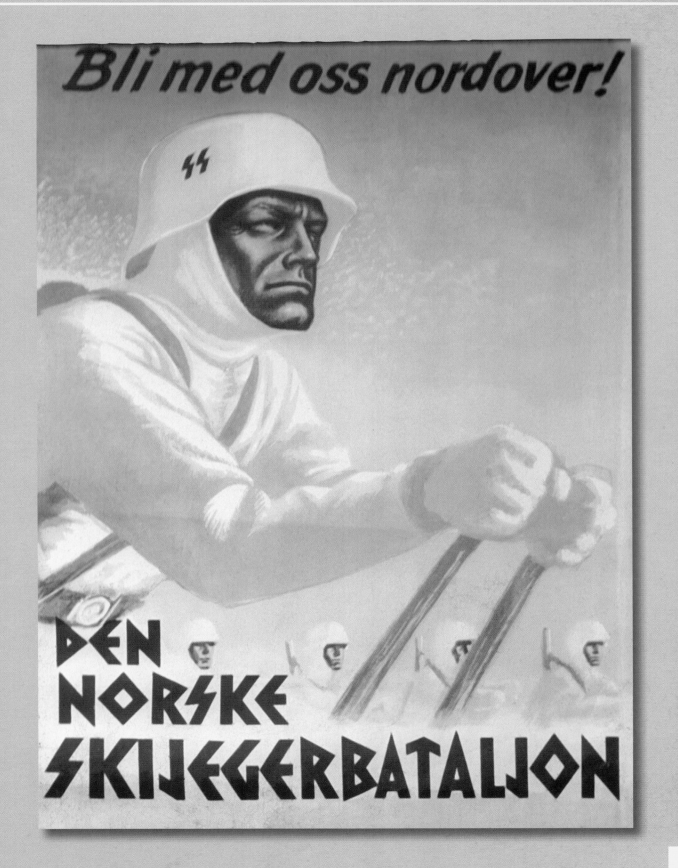

Forced Labour

Such numbers were dwarfed by the millions of people forced to work against their will. In the first year of the war, 1939, the Germans shipped more than 300,000 forced workers to Germany, mainly from Poland. Some Germans were reluctant to allow Slavs into the country – the Germans saw them as subhuman people – but economic demands overcame ideology.

There were further large intakes of labourers following the fall of France in 1940 and the invasion of Russia in Operation Barbarossa in June 1941. Early in that campaign, many Russian prisoners were murdered before they even reached Germany, but things changed after spring 1942, as workers became more valuable. In all, some 2.5 million Soviet prisoners were deported to Germany.

Working for Germany

By 1944, when the demands of maintaining the war effort had strained the German economy to breaking point, overseas workers made up nearly a quarter of the German workforce. More than 5.2 million foreign conscripts joined with 1.8 million prisoners of war to keep German industry and agriculture going. The workers lived in 20,000 work camps that had been built throughout the country. Many of the workforce from

FELLES FRONT MOT BOLSJEVISMEN

⇐ **The flags included on this SS recruiting poster show those of various western European nations, including Denmark and Belgium, that contributed soldiers to what it describes as a 'United Front Against Bolshevism'.**

FOREIGN LEGIONS OF THE SS

In 1941 Adolf Hitler was convinced by his commanders to allow non-German volunteers to join the Waffen-SS. The military elite was the armed wing of the Nazi Party. Hitler doubted that recruits would be of high enough quality, but two new regiments were rapidly formed: Nordland, of Danes and Norwegians, and Westland, with Dutch and Flemish soldiers. Nazi ideology attracted so many enthusiastic volunteers from throughout occupied Europe that a special training camp had to be opened to accommodate them all.

⟹ Watched by a German guard, Ukrainian women spin wool to make winter clothing for German forces. The Germans forced whole villages into working for them.

western Europe were employed in industrial jobs, where they received the best food and generally better treatment. Those from the east, particularly Poles, were send to work in agriculture, which reflected their more lowly status in German eyes. Agricultural labourers were worked hard and treated so badly that many of them fell sick or died. Their diet consisted almost entirely of vegetables and a little bread; meat was a rare luxury.

WANNSEE CONFERENCE

In 1942 senior Nazis met in the Wannsee suburb of Berlin to agree a 'final solution' as to how to treat Europe's Jews. They adopted a plan to send all Jews to Poland, either to endure forced labour or for extermination in the death camps.

Jewish Workers

By 1944 the Germans needed yet more workers. The loss of occupied territory to the Allies was reducing the amount of workers available. This time they turned to the concentration camps where, since 1938, the SS had interned Jews, political enemies of the Nazis, Roma and others, including homosexuals, on a large scale. By the end of 1944 some 700,000 prisoners were held in the camps. They

constituted a valuable source of labour.

It was already common for camps to use prisoners to run their own industrial ventures. Now economic need brought the system under the control of Berlin. The minister for armaments and munitions, Albert Speer, was busy reforming the economy to make sure that war needs could be met. Late in 1942 he ordered the SS to release inmates from concentration camps to work in industry.

OUR FLAG
IS GOING FORWARD TOO

⇐ **The Germans even tried to raise recruits from among British prisoners of war: about 60 volunteered for the 'British Free Corps'.**

⇓ **Prisoners make armaments in a workshop in the concentration camp at Dachau in 1943.**

Over the next two years the numbers of prisoners working outside the camps rose rapidly. To begin with, they included few Jews; however, by 1944, despite the decision at the Wannsee Conference in 1942 to exterminate all Jews (see page 31), more and more were being diverted to work for the Germans. Some 600,000 inmates (including non-Jews) were working by late 1944.

The work performed by the slave labourers varied. Often, however, the concentration camp workers were employed on special projects, such as digging underground tunnels, building factories or even running printing presses to manufacture fake Allied currency. The conditions were usually harsh and the food barely adequate. Workers were pushed so hard by their guards that many

were worked to death. Others were beaten or even killed as punishments for minor infringements of discipline.

One remarkable story from the work camps was that of Oskar Schindler (see box, right). Schindler was an industrialist who originally employed Jewish workers from the camps because they were cheap. However, he became concerned for the welfare of his workers – now known as Schindler's Jews – and used his own fortune to save them from being sent to the death camps.

Nazi Fighters

Among the most unusual 'workers' for the Germans were the thousands of foreigners who chose to enlist in the German armed forces. During the 1930s the fascist beliefs of Hitler and Mussolini had gained supporters throughout Europe. Some countries occupied by the Germans, such as the Netherlands, had well-established fascist parties of their own. Their members volunteered to fight to spread the ideology. In former Soviet regions, meanwhile, ethnically non-Russian populations had suffered under Stalin's dictatorship in the 1930s. Now Ukrainians, Belorussians and Latvians were all eager to join the Germans to fight their former oppressors.

The most committed Nazis joined the Waffen SS, the combat units of the Nazi Party. There was even a small British SS detachment, recruited from among prisoners of war. Altogether, there were some 21 foreign divisions, which provided the Germans with a great propaganda coup. The recruits came from the Low Countries, Scandinavia, Italy, Hungary, Russia and other countries.

⇦ **This staircase in the factory owned by Oskar Schindler was famous as a way for workers to reach safety by becoming one of 'Schindler's Jews'.**

OSKAR SCHINDLER

Oskar Schindler was a German industrialist who owned factories in Poland and the Czech Republic. Schindler used Jewish forced labourers to work for him. Although he was friendly with many senior SS officers, Schindler was appalled at the treatment of the Jews. He went out of his way to protect his 1,000 workers and their families and paid bribes to officials to leave them alone. He claimed that they were essential for the war effort. Near the end of the war he moved his workers to what is now the Czech Republic. That way he saved them from certain death.

⇦ **Oskar Schindler's grave in Jerusalem is piled with stones, left by visitors as a traditional Jewish sign of gratitude.**

Resistance

Many people living in occupied countries in Europe and Asia bitterly resented the occupiers. They resisted their rule in a wide range of ways, including with violent attacks.

The most famous resistance movement, the French Resistance, or Maquis, fought an armed guerrilla campaign against the Germans. In European countries such as Yugoslavia and, later, Italy and in the Philippines in Asia similar armed partisan movements attacked occupying forces before retreating to hideouts in remote regions.

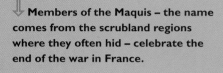

Members of the Maquis – the name comes from the scrubland regions where they often hid – celebrate the end of the war in France.

A Dangerous Game

Armed movements were only a small, but important, part of resistance. They required great courage. Most resistance fighters who were caught were executed, often after being tortured for information about their colleagues. Resistance activity was also often met with severe acts of reprisal. In Russia, for example, the death of one German in a resistance attack might lead to the deaths of hundreds of randomly selected men, women and children.

This Free French poster was designed to encourage British support for French resistance to the 'Boche', a slang term for Germans. In reality, the Resistance only had much effect on the Germans from 1944.

FRENCH RESISTANCE

The French resistance played a vital role in the run-up to D-Day, the Allied landing in France in June 1944. Resistance groups not only spied for the Allies, who knew the location of all the German defences; they also blew up miles of railway lines in order to prevent the Germans moving supplies and reinforcements to meet the invasion. As the Allies advanced on Paris, thousands of Parisians took up arms and began to fight the German authorities, helping to liberate their own city.

PARTISANS

Partisans differed from other resistance movements. They were unofficial military forces, with military command structures, discipline and uniforms. They were often made up of former soldiers. Important partisan movements were formed in Russia by Red Army soldiers caught behind German lines; in Yugoslavia by soldiers who fled to the mountains after the German invasion; and in Italy after the German occupation of the north of the country.

⇑ **Women, as well as former regular soldiers, joined the Partisan forces led by Tito in Yugoslavia.**

Around the world far more people demonstrated their rejection of occupation simply by making it as awkward as possible for the Axis forces to govern them. This form of demonstration was more difficult to punish because it was harder to prove.

MESSAGES FROM BRITAIN

The British Special Operations Executive coordinated resistance within France through a system of agents and radio messages. The agents parachuted into France with wireless sets that could be used to listen to messages from London. At various times in their schedule, the BBC broadcast a stream of odd sentences that contained pre-arranged messages aimed at different resistance groups. They contained instructions about what the groups should do and when they should do it.

Filipinos kept their children away from school, for example, in protest against lessons that were being taught in Japanese. Meanwhile, Europeans secretly painted large 'V' signs on walls as a symbol for 'victory'. It was first used in Belgium but had been popularised by the British prime minister Winston Churchill. The sign helped to reassure Europeans of continuing opposition to the Germans.

Some groups printed underground anti-German newspapers on illegal presses and distributed them in secret. Although anyone involved with the newspaper risked punishment including execution, some resistance papers had a circulation of hundreds of thousands.

Secret Services

The British and American secret services (the Special Operations Executive, SOE, and the Office of Strategic Services,

⬅ **A member of the Dutch resistance takes down messages over a radio: possession of a radio set could be punished by death.**

OSS, respectively) supplied equipment to resistance movements. They also sent agents to organise sabotage missions and spying activities that kept the Allied informed about German activity.

Armed Resistance

Armed resistance grew. In Norway, for example, the movement gained 40,000 members, many trained by the British. Their most significant action was the blowing up of a factory in 1943 that was a vital part of Germany's plan to develop an atomic bomb.

In France, resistance grew after 1942, when civilians fleeing deportation to Germany escaped into the French countryside. They formed resistance groups and took the name Maquis, from the name given to the scrubland of southern France. They mounted sabotage and assassination campaigns against the invaders throughout the country.

SABOTAGE

One of the most effective resistance tactics was sabotage, or the deliberate destruction of property or equipment. Railway lines and road and rail bridges could be blown up by relatively small bombs, which were easy to store and carry, but which still disrupted enemy operations severely.

⟹ **This explosive device is positioned to destroy a railway track.**

THE FILIPINOS

Japan's occupation of the Philippines left large areas where guerrilla movements took root. The most powerful was the People's Anti-Japanese Army (PAJA), or Hukbalahap, which attacked enemy bases. The PAJA was motivated in part by its communist sympathies. The growth of communist power would have major consequences for Southeast Asia after the war.

Resistance in the East

Further east, huge resistance movements flourished in Poland, Russia and Yugoslavia. The Germans faced two full-scale uprisings in the Polish capital, Warsaw, in 1943 and 1944, both of which were crushed by occupation forces.

In Russia and Yugoslavia, resistance was mainly in the hands of partisan forces made up of former soldiers. In Russia, Stalin's secret service, the NKVD, also organised resistance groups – often by terrorising Russian civilians into taking part despite their fear of German reprisals.

Yugoslavia's partisans were divided among royalists and communists and they began a bitter civil war between themselves. Eventually the royalists made an alliance with the Germans to fight their common enemy – but it was the

⇐ **'Defend our beloved Moscow': this 1941 Soviet poster sums up the desperate call for resistance as the Germans approached to within a few miles of the walls of the capital.**

NKVD

Stalin used the NKVD to detain and execute enemies and to run internal prison camps. In the war, the NKVD sometimes treated Russian civilians as harshly as the Germans did in order to guarantee their continued resistance to occupation.

COASTWATCHERS

One role of resistance movements in Asia was to provide intelligence about the movement of Japanese forces. Even before the war broke out, the Royal Australian Navy had organised networks of 'coastwatchers'. In 1942 and 1943, in particular, these Australian and New Zealand agents, plus many local volunteers, reported on Japanese activity along thousands of miles of island coast in the Pacific. They allowed the Allies to build up an overall picture of Japanese movements.

⇑ **The coastwatchers' intimate knowledge of the Pacific islands enabled them to follow any unusual Japanese activity inland or at sea.**

communists led by Josip Broz, better known as Tito, who emerged victorious and formed the postwar government.

Resistance to Japan

In Asia, resistance to Japanese occupation varied from passive gestures on the part of individuals to full-blown guerrilla warfare. Passive gestures were more common because of the efficiency of Japanese rule, which was brutal in its treatment of suspected resisters. Both the British and the Americans provided training and arms for guerrillas in Asia, although it was difficult to provide a consistent stream of supplies. The U.S. Office of Strategic Services (OSS), set up to coordinate resistance and gather intelligence from occupied countries, trained resistance fighters in Thailand and Burma, as well as communist guerrillas in Indochina.

The British Special Operations Executive (SOE) taught resistance fighters in Singapore, Burma and Malaya (now Malaysia). The most successful movement emerged in Malaya, where the Malayan People's Anti-Japanese Army reached a total of about 7,000 members, who constantly attacked and harried Japanese soldiers and officials.

⇓ **A Japanese submarine surfaces. Coastwatchers reported the movements of Japanese naval vessels.**

The Holocaust

The Nazis used their occupation of most of Europe to attempt to exterminate those they saw as 'undesirables'. They murdered some six million people, most of whom were Jews.

Germany, like other parts of central and eastern Europe, had a long history of anti-Semitism, or prejudice against Jews. In his reaction to the country's defeat in World War I and the economic crisis that followed, Adolf Hitler had openly blamed the Jews for causing the country's problems. He suggested that greedy Jewish bankers were part of an international plot to make huge profits at the expense of ordinary Germans.

A Popular Message

Hitler's message was a popular one. After the Nazis formed the government in 1933 they passed a series of laws that discriminated against Jews. Jews were forbidden to marry non-Jews, for example. They were barred from professional jobs, for example in law or accountancy. Jewish businesses were handed to non-Jews. Jews were also forced to wear a yellow star as a badge to identify themselves. They were regularly beaten up in the street by Nazis.

⇒ **A railway line leads through the main gate of the death camp at Auschwitz-Birkenau, the largest of the Nazis' concentration camps. Some three million people died at the camp.**

GYPSIES

The Roma, or Romani, and the Sinti were ancient European ethnic minorities who lived in often nomadic communities. Sometimes referred to as gypsies, they were concentrated in central and eastern Europe. Seeing them as coming from inferior races, the Nazis targeted gypsies alongside Jews for extermination. They were killed by death squads in the occupied Soviet Union or sent to extermination camps. There are few records of gypsy numbers before the war, so it is difficult to calculate how many gypsies died. Reliable estimates put the number at between 220,000 and 500,000 dead.

⇑ **A railway goods wagon used during the deportation of European Jews now stands in place as a memorial to victims of the Holocaust.**

ANTI-SEMITISM

Germany and other European countries had a tradition of hostility toward Jews. People found Jewish religion and culture strange. They were also suspicious of the Jews' reputation as moneylenders and businessmen.

In November 1938, Hitler ordered *Kristallnacht*, or the Night of Broken Glass. Nazi stormtroopers attacked thousands of Jewish businesses and synagogues, breaking windows and doing much more serious damage. Many Germans were horrified at the thuggish violence. The Nazis realised that they had gone too far for many of their citizens. From now on, they would mainly tackle the Jewish 'problem' in secret.

⇑ **Deported Jews stare out from a closed railway wagon during their journey across Europe.**

Before the outbreak of war in 1939 the Nazis had forcefully encouraged many Jews to leave Germany (they were forced to abandon their possessions, which then became the property of the state). Around half of all Germany's Jews had emigrated before the war began.

Advance to the East

The situation changed as Germany advanced to the east. Countries there, particularly Poland and parts of the Soviet Union, were home to millions of Jews living in long-established communities. The Nazis believed that these Jews were inferior even to the Jews in Germany. They were determined to get rid of them. When the Germans invaded Poland, more than 2.5 million Jews came under their rule. The Nazis herded them into small ghettos, closed areas in which they lived in crowded poverty.

The Final Solution

In June 1941, when the Germans invaded the Soviet Union, even more Jews came under their control. Hitler had specified that the war in Russia was a war for survival. The enemy should be shown no mercy. The German troops were

ANNE FRANK

Anne Frank's diary is a record of the Holocaust through the eyes of Europe's Jews. She wrote it during two years while her family hid from the Nazis in Amsterdam in a secret apartment above a warehouse office. Anne's diary recorded the family's difficult life, but also included her optimistic hopes for the future. She worked hard at her studies because she wanted to become a journalist. In August 1944 the whole family was betrayed to the Gestapo and sent to concentration camps. Anne died in captivity in Bergen-Belsen in March 1945. Only Anne's father survived. After the war, he returned to the secret apartment, where he discovered his daughter's diary on the floor.

LIBERATING BERGEN–BELSEN

The concentration camp at Bergen–Belsen in northwestern Germany was liberated by British troops on 15 April, 1945. Even though it was not a death camp, the shocked soldiers found some 10,000 dead bodies, most of whom had died from starvation or typhus. There were 60,000 survivors, some of whom were so ill that they died soon afterwards. The liberators moved the prisoners and forced the SS guards to bury the dead. Then they used flamethrowers to burn Bergen–Belsen to the ground.

⇑ **A British officer reads the sign marking the position of Bergen–Belsen after the camp was destroyed by the Allies.**

accompanied by *Einsatzgruppen*, or 'task forces'. These Gestapo death squads killed Jews in large numbers: perhaps 500,000 by the end of 1941 and up to two million by the end of the war.

At a conference held in the Berlin suburb of Wannsee in January 1942, Nazi leaders agreed what they called 'the final solution to the Jewish question'. The policy was actually created by the Reich security chief Reinhard Heydrich. The Nazis would no longer try to expel Jews from Germany and occupied territories. Instead, they would send them to Poland to be used as forced labour – and worked to death if necessary – or exterminated in death camps.

⇓ **These crematorium ovens were used to dispose of dead bodies at the Dachau camp in Germany.**

The Death Camps

The Nazis had begun to imprison Jews and other groups, including their political opponents, in concentration camps within Germany from 1933. Now they moved to a policy of deliberate extermination at small camps built especially for the purpose. The camps were built outside Germany, so that people would not know what was going on there.

Initially three death camps were constructed, at Belzec, Sobibor and Treblinka in Poland; they began operating in March 1942. Later death camps included the infamous Auschwitz-Birkenau, which was also a work camp.

Jews were sent to the death camps by train from various parts of occupied Europe. Some European governments resisted deporting the Jews. Those in Bulgaria, Finland and Hungary – until it was occupied by the Germans in 1944 – refused to cooperate. Many individuals bravely hid Jews in their homes. In countries such as Lithuania, Ukraine and Romania, however, large sections of the local population willingly helped deport their Jewish neighbours.

Death on a Huge Scale

When the closed trains arrived at the death camps, the new arrivals usually

⇑ **Argentine Jews protest at denials of the Holocaust made by the Iranian president Mahmoud Ahmadinejad in 2005.**

had only hours to live. They were placed in an assembly area and divided into men and women. Both groups were forced to strip, so that Jewish aids at the camp could sort through their clothes and remove anything valuable. Women often had their heads shaved so that their hair could be used as mattress stuffing. The prisoners were told that they would be given a shower and they were marched into a chamber. Once the room was full, the doors were locked and cans of deadly Zyklon B gas were dropped in. The dead bodies were then thrown into mass graves or burned in crematorium ovens.

Work Camps

Not all Jews were sent to extermination camps. Some were put to work in camps that had work places, such as factories and quarries. Nevertheless, the prisoners were subject to inhuman treatment. They were kept near starvation and many died from exhaustion. Others were simply

Eyewitness

RICHARD DIMBLEBY

Richard Dimbleby was a reporter for the British Broadcasting Service (BBC) when he accompanied the soldiers who liberated the concentration camp at Bergen–Belsen on 15 April, 1945.

'Here over an acre of ground lay dead and dying people. You could not see which was which…. The living lay with their heads against the corpses and around them moved the awful, ghostly procession of emaciated, aimless people, with nothing to do and with no hope of life, unable to move out of your way, unable to look at the terrible sights around them…. This day at Belsen was the most horrible of my life.'

HOLOCAUST DENIERS

A tiny handful of people insist that the Holocaust did not take place. They include a few historians but most are people who sympathise with fascist ideas. They argue that the Jews have made up the story, despite all the evidence to the contrary. The vast majority of experts reject their ideas. In many countries in Europe – including Germany – it is a crime to deny the Holocaust.

executed by prison guards or died during so-called medical experiments performed by Nazi doctors.

In all some six million Jews died during what became known as the 'Holocaust', from Greek words meaning a burned sacrifice. They were not the only victims, however. The Germans also rounded up and killed the minority Roma and Sinti, who mainly lived in eastern Europe and the Balkans. Up to 15,000 homosexuals were murdered, along with thousands of communists.

> " *The Holocaust is a central event in many people's lives, but it also has become a metaphor for our century.* "
>
> **AHARON APPELFELD**

Walking through the canyons of the Berlin Holocaust Memorial is a disorientating experience. It is difficult to see what is ahead, and the sloping ground makes walking hazardous.

MEMORIALS

Many countries now have Holocaust memorials. They think that they are the best way to remember the victims of the Nazis – and to ensure that such an event does not happen again. One of the most recent memorials opened in Berlin itself in 2005. Designed by U.S. architect Peter Eisenman, it is a basin the size of a city block filled with 2,711 granite blocks that rise to over 4 metres (13 feet). Visitors walk through narrow channels between the blocks, down into the deepest canyons and back out again.

Refugees

During the war, many people fled the fighting and became refugees. At the end of the conflict, the problem became even worse as millions of people tried to find new homes.

The early fighting in the war already created refugees in France, Belgium and Poland as people fled to avoid the fighting or to abandon homes and businesses that had been destroyed. Jews had meanwhile begun fleeing Nazi persecution within Germany, although many sought refuge in countries that later also came under German control.

Movement of Populations

The full extent of the refugee problem facing Europe only became apparent at the end of the war, however. One estimate is that Europe had 40 million refugees in what was the largest movement of populations the continent has ever seen.

REFUGEES

In World War II, refugees who had been forced from their homes were usually referred to as Displaced Persons. The term also included prisoners and slave labourers.

⬇ **Early in the war, French refugees flee to escape the German advance into the northeast of France.**

➡ **This Dutch poster from before the war calls for contributions to help Jews fleeing the Nazis in Germany. These refugees had lost their homes, jobs and possessions in the process.**

UNITED NATIONS

The United Nations Relief and Rehabilitation Administration (UNRRA) was set up in 1943 to help get displaced persons (DPs) home. It became the International Refugee Organisation in 1946 and the UN High Commission for Refugees in 1950.

The people on the move included former prisoners of war and forced labourers who were returning home from Germany. There were hundreds of thousands of Jews who had survived the concentration camps. Meanwhile, however, there were also many Germans who were making their way back from 'Greater Germany'.

Many minority groups found that the end of the fighting did not bring the end

⇒ **French children hold American flags in 1946, having just received part of a Red Cross shipment of chocolate and sweets.**

EAST PRUSSIA

East Prussia, a region on the Baltic, was separated from Germany itself by former Polish territory. As Soviet forces advanced, most of East Prussia's 2.2 million Germans fled west. Some had little idea of how badly the war was going for Germany until the last minute. Reports of Russians massacring civilians and raping women caused widespread panic. Many refugees drowned when Soviet submarines sank three passenger ships in the Baltic. After a four-day battle the regional capital at Königsberg fell to the Red Army. The population dropped to only 195,000 at the end of the war. Some Germans returned later but found themselves deported to the Soviet Union.

RED CROSS

The Red Cross took on a major role in trying to locate refugees and to help prisoners of war to return home. However, as the Soviet Union was not a signatory to the Geneva Convention, it did not allow the Red Cross to operate. That made it difficult to track down vast numbers of refugees stranded in what was now Soviet-run territory.

of their suffering. They often faced prejudice from the communities by which they found themselves surrounded. The Poles, for example, forcibly deported some of the Germans in their country.

Fate of the Volksdeutsch

Germans living in countries that had come under Soviet control, such as Czechoslovakia, were sent deeper into Soviet territory to provide slave labour. Others were deported to Germany. The 2.2 million Germans expelled from Czechoslovakia had their property

→ **Women workers rebuild the Berlin underground railway in 1945. German troops had destroyed much of the system to prevent Russian forces advancing through the tunnels.**

confiscated. In Yugoslavia, meanwhile, Germans were also expelled or were put in camps or sent to the Soviet Union.

The German deportees included people who had arrived in other countries recently, encouraged by the Nazi expansion of 'Greater Germany'. But some of these Volksdeutsch belonged to families that had lived in places such as Hungary for generations.

In all, up to 11.5 million Germans left or were expelled from eastern European countries in the five years after the end of the war. Some 600,000 may have died in the accompanying violence.

Back to the Soviet Union

Soviet prisoners held in Germany, meanwhile, were often condemned as traitors by Stalin's government. Some 1.5 million of them were returned to the Soviet Union but there were sent into

REBUILDING BERLIN

With so many men dead – there were seven million more women than men in Germany – and up to 30 per cent of central Berlin destroyed by Allied bombing or fighting, the Allies conscripted German women to take on the work of clearing and rebuilding the city. All women aged between 15 and 50 were liable to be conscripted in 1945 and 1946. These Trümmerfrau ('rubble women') had little equipment. They used picks and hammers to demolish buildings. The bricks and any other features such as doors were cleaned and then used for new construction work.

internal exile in the infamous gulags (prison camps) of Siberia.

More of the 5 million former Soviet citizens in western Europe were sent back to the Soviet Union against their will. They included even people who had settled in Europe before the war and who had become citizens of other countries.

Their deportation was part of a deal concerning the postwar government of German-occupied territory that was agreed at Yalta in February 1945. Soviet leader Joseph Stalin had forced Britain and the United States to agree to deport Soviet citizens, despite Stalin's record of persecuting his political opponents.

The Jews and Israel

Many Jews who were liberated from the concentration camps were unwelcome in their former homelands. There was still deep prejudice against them. In Poland and Slovakia their former neighbours attacked them – and even killed them. About 100,000 Jews fled to Allied-administered territory, where they lived in camps for displaced persons (DPs).

Many wished to travel to Palestine, the ancient homeland of the Jews. Since the late 1800s Jews had settled there with the aim of creating a Jewish state. However, the British who governed

> *I had faith in Israel before it was established; I have [faith] in it now.*
> **HARRY S. TRUMAN**

Eyewitness

CHARLES LINDBERGH

Aviator Charles Lindbergh entered Germany with the U.S. Army at the end of the war. He described the process of occupation.

'When our army moves into an occupied village, the most desirable houses are selected and the occupants ordered out. They are permitted to take their clothing and certain household utensils and furniture – not essential furniture or beds. Where they go for food or shelter is considered none of the conquering army's concern.'

Palestine tried to limit Jewish immigration in order to prevent conflict between Jews and the Arabs who had also lived there for thousands of years. It was only with the creation of the State of Israel in 1948 that many Jewish refugees were able to finally leave Europe.

Returning the DPs

At the end of the war Europe had more than 40 million refugees. Some seven million of these displaced persons or DPs

⇐ **The chapel at Valchevrière in the Alps of southwestern France is one of many memorials in Europe to villages that were destroyed by German reprisals for resistance activity: the inhabitants were either killed or displaced.**

↑ **Women in Tokyo help clear rubble after the Japanese surrender. Many citizens had been displaced by Allied bombing raids.**

were quickly sent back to their countries of origin with the help of the United Nations Relief and Rehabilitation Administration (UNRRA), which was set up in 1943 to help displaced people.

While they waited to be repatriated, DPs lived in camps. These barracks or tent cities were often set up by the military but then usually taken over by UNRRA. Camps often had facilities such as schools. A tracking bureau worked with the Red Cross to try to track down other survivors.

Some groups of DPs could not go home because they faced persecution. They included Jews from eastern Europe, but also peoples whose homelands had fallen under Soviet control in the Baltic or elsewhere, or which were under communist control in Yugoslavia.

Between 1945 and 1953 various countries volunteered to take refugees from the DP camps. Israel took 650,000 and the United States 600,000. Other volunteer nations included the United Kingdom, France, Canada, Belgium and Australia. Critics accused their goverments of looking for cheap labour.

Of the 250,000 DPs still in camps by 1953, most were eventually accepted as citizens by Germany and Austria.

WAR CHILDREN

After five years of war, many children in occupied Europe had German fathers. There were some 8,000 in Demark, as many as 200,000 in France and up to 50,000 in the Netherlands. In Norway, the 12,000 'war children' were partly the result of a Nazi programme to encourage soldiers to have racially pure children (the Germans saw Norwegians as similar to themselves). These so-called 'war children' and their mothers were often treated harshly after the war and faced severe discrimination.

Timeline of World War II

1939

SEPTEMBER:

German troops invade and overrun Poland

Britain and France declare war on Germany

The Soviet Union invades eastern Poland and extends control to the Baltic states

The Battle of the Atlantic begins

NOVEMBER:

The Soviet Union launches a winter offensive against Finland

1940

APRIL:

Germany invades Denmark and Norway

Allied troops land in Norway

MAY:

Germany invades Luxembourg, the Netherlands, Belgium and France

Allied troops are evacuated at Dunkirk

JUNE:

Italy declares war on France and Britain

German troops enter Paris

France signs an armistice with Germany

Italy bombs Malta in the Mediterranean

JULY:

German U-boats inflict heavy losses on Allied convoys in the Atlantic

Britain sends warships to neutralise the French fleet in North Africa

The Battle of Britain begins

SEPTEMBER:

Luftwaffe air raids begin the Blitz – the bombing of London and other British cities

Italian troops advance from Libya into Egypt

Germany, Italy and Japan sign the Tripartite Pact

OCTOBER:

Italy invades Greece; Greek forces, aided by the British, mount a counterattack

DECEMBER:

British troops at Sidi Barrani, Egypt, force the Italians to retreat

1941

JANUARY:

Allied units capture Tobruk in Libya

British forces in Sudan attack Italian East Africa

FEBRUARY:

Allies defeat Italy at Benghazi, Libya

Rommel's Afrika Korps arrive in Tripoli

MARCH:

The Africa Korps drive British troops back from El Agheila

APRIL:

German, Italian and Hungarian units invade Yugoslavia

German forces invade Greece

The Afrika Korps beseige Tobruk

MAY:

The British sink the German battleship *Bismarck*

JUNE:

German troops invade the Soviet Union

JULY:

German forces advance to within 16 kilometres (10 miles) of Kiev

AUGUST:

The United States bans the export of oil to Japan

SEPTEMBER:

German forces start the siege of Leningrad

German Army Group Centre advances on Moscow

NOVEMBER:

British troops begin an attack to relieve Tobruk

The Allies liberate Ethiopia

DECEMBER:

Japanese aircraft attack the U.S. Pacific Fleet at Pearl Harbor

Japan declares war on the United States and Britain

The United States, Britain and the Free French declare war on Japan

Japanese forces invade the Philippines, Malaya and Thailand, and defeat the British garrison in Hong Kong

1942

JANUARY:

Japan attacks the Dutch East Indies and invades Burma

Rommel launches a new offensive in Libya

FEBRUARY:
Singapore surrenders to the Japanese
APRIL:
The Bataan Peninsula in the Philippines falls to the Japanese
MAY:
U.S. and Japanese fleets clash at the Battle of the Coral Sea
Rommel attacks the Gazala Line in Libya
JUNE:
The U.S. Navy defeats the Japanese at the Battle of Midway
Rommel recaptures Tobruk and the Allies retreat to Egypt
JULY:
The Germans take Sebastopol after a long siege and advance into the Caucasus
AUGUST:
U.S. Marines encounter fierce Japanese resistance in the Solomons
SEPTEMBER–OCTOBER:
Allied forces defeat Axis troops at El Alamein, Egypt – the first major Allied victory of the war
NOVEMBER:
U.S. and British troops land in Morocco and Algeria

1943

FEBRUARY:
The German Sixth Army surrenders at Stalingrad
The Japanese evacuate troops from Guadalcanal in the Solomons
MAY:
Axis forces in Tunisia surrender, ending the campaign in North Africa
JULY:
U.S. troops make landings on New Georgia Island in the Solomons
The Red Army wins the Battle of Kursk
Allied troops land on Sicily
British bombers conduct massive raids on Hamburg
AUGUST:
German forces occupy Italy
SEPTEMBER:
Allied units begin landings on mainland Italy
Italy surrenders, prompting a German invasion of northern Italy
OCTOBER:
The Red Army liberates the Caucasus
NOVEMBER:
U.S. carrier aircraft attack Rabaul in the Solomons

1944

JANUARY:
The German siege of Leningrad ends
FEBRUARY:
U.S. forces conquer the Marshall Islands

MARCH:
The Soviet offensive reaches the Dniester River
Allied aircraft bomb the monastery at Monte Cassino in Italy
JUNE:
U.S. troops enter the city of Rome
D-Day–the Allies begin the invasion of northern Europe
U.S. aircraft defeat the Japanese fleet at the Battle of the Philippine Sea
JULY:
The Red Army begins its offensive to clear the Baltic states
Soviet tanks enter Poland
AUGUST:
Japanese troops withdraw from Myitkyina in Burma
French forces liberate Paris
Allied units liberate towns in France, Belgium and the Netherlands
OCTOBER:
Soviet and Yugoslavian troops capture Belgrade, the Yugoslav capital
The Japanese suffer defeat at the Battle of Leyte Gulf
DECEMBER:
Hitler counterattacks in the Ardennes in the Battle of the Bulge

1945

JANUARY:
The U.S. Army lands on Luzon in the Philippines
The Red Army liberates Auschwitz
Most of Poland and Czechoslovakia are liberated by the Allies
FEBRUARY:
U.S. troops take the Philippine capital, Manila
U.S. Marines land on the island of Iwo Jima
Soviet troops strike west across Germany
The U.S. Army heads towards the River Rhine
APRIL:
U.S. troops land on the island of Okinawa
Mussolini is shot by partisans
Soviet troops assault Berlin
Hitler commits suicide in his bunker
MAY:
All active German forces surrender
JUNE:
Japanese resistance ends in Burma and on Okinawa
AUGUST:
Atomic bombs are dropped on Hiroshima and Nagasaki
Japan surrenders

World War II: Europe

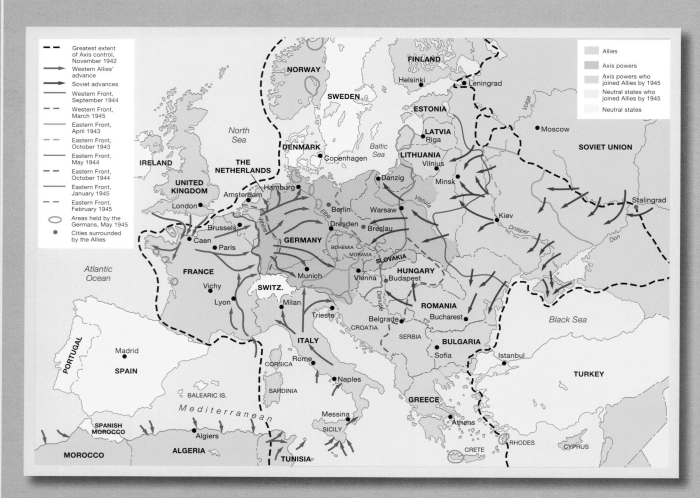

Legend:
- Greatest extent of Axis control, November 1942
- Western Allies' advance
- Soviet advances
- Western Front, September 1944
- Western Front, March 1945
- Eastern Front, April 1943
- Eastern Front, October 1943
- Eastern Front, May 1944
- Eastern Front, October 1944
- Eastern Front, January 1945
- Eastern Front, February 1945
- Areas held by the Germans, May 1945
- Cities surrounded by the Allies

- Allies
- Axis powers
- Axis powers who joined Allies by 1945
- Neutral states who joined Allies by 1945
- Neutral states

The war began with rapid German advances through the Low Countries and northern France. In June 1941 German armies struck through eastern Europe into the Soviet Union, besieging Leningrad and Stalingrad. However, Allied landings in North Africa led to eventual victory there and opened the way for the invasion of Sicily and then of the Italian peninsula itself, forcing Italy to surrender. In the east the defeat of the German Sixth Army at Stalingrad forced a long retreat during which German forces were harried by communist guerrillas at all moments. In June 1944 Allied forces landed in northern France on D-Day and began to fight their way towards Berlin. As the Soviet advance closed in and the Americans and British crossed the Rhine River into Germany, defeat became inevitable. Hitler committed suicide in his bunker at the heart of his failed Reich, or empire.

World War II: The Pacific

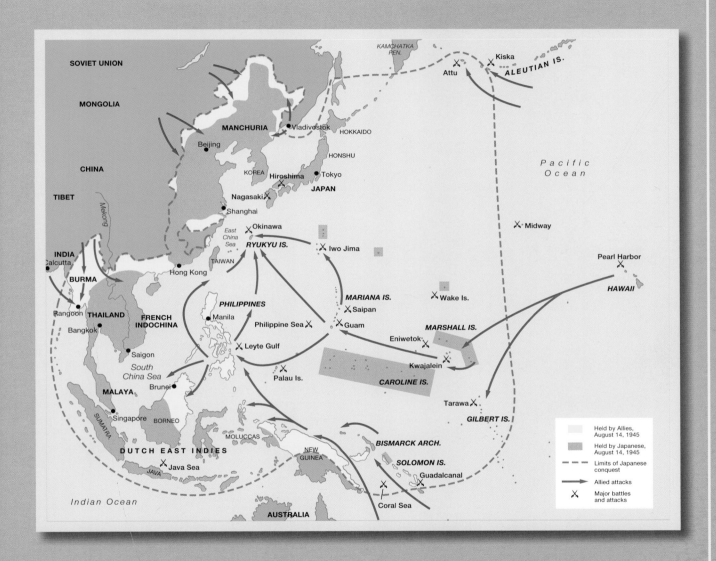

The Pacific conflict began with swift Japanese advances and occupation of territory throughout Southeast Asia, Malaya, the East Indies, the Philippines and the island groups of the Pacific. The U.S. fleet was weakened by the attack on Pearl Harbor, but the damage it suffered was repaired remarkably quickly. After the naval victory at Midway in June 1942, U.S. commanders fought a campaign of 'island hopping', overcoming strong local Japanese resistance to establish a series of stepping stones that would bring their bombers close enough to attack the Japanese home islands. Meanwhile, British and Indian troops pushed back the Japanese advance from Burma.

Biographies

Neville Chamberlain

British statesman. Conservative prime minister from 1937 to 1940, Chamberlain led the policy of appeasement of Hitler. He argued that giving in to Hitler's demands was the best way to prevent war. When the policy failed, he resigned in favour of Winston Churchill.

Churchill, Winston

British statesman. Churchill became British prime minister in May 1940 after a controversial political career. He was an energetic, inspiring and imaginative leader. His powerful speeches and his careful cultivation of Britain's U.S. allies were vital to the Allies' war effort. After the war's end Churchill was defeated in a general election, but he later became prime minister again in 1951.

De Gaulle, Charles

French statesman. French army officer De Gaulle escaped to London after the German invasion of France in 1939 and set up the Free French to oppose the Vichy regime's collaboration with Germany. Under De Gaulle's leadership, the Free French grew to include some 300,000 fighters, including partisans of the French Resistance. In 1945 he was elected president of France and later founded the Fifth Republic.

Eisenhower, Dwight D.

U.S. general. Eisenhower was part of the U.S. war plans division when he was promoted in June 1942 to become commander of U.S. forces in Europe. He led the Allied landings in North Africa and Sicily and the capture of Rome. As supreme commander of Allied forces, he led the D-Day landings in northern France and the liberation of Paris and advance into Germany. His popularity was reflected by his election in 1952 as the 34th president of the United States, a position he held for 12 years.

Goebbels, Joseph

Nazi leader. Joseph Goebbels was the head of Nazi Party propaganda and later became minister of propaganda in the Nazi government. He used mass media and cinema skilfully to promote Nazi views. At the end of the war, he killed his children and committed suicide with his wife.

Hirohito

Emperor of Japan. Hirohito reluctantly approved the growth of army power and the militarization of Japanese society. He also backed the aggressive foreign policy that eventually led to war, but in 1945 he supported the leaders who wanted to surrender unconditionally. After the war he gave up his divine status and became a constitutional monarch.

Hitler, Adolf

Dictator of Germany. After serving as a soldier in World War I, Adolf Hitler joined a minor political party that he renamed the National Socialist Workers' Party (Nazis). Hitler was elected as chancellor of Germany in 1933 and became leader (Führer) in 1934. His policies were based on anti-Semitism and anti-communism, militarism and the aggressive expansion of Germany. His invasion of Poland in September 1939 sparked the outbreak of the war. Hitler's war leadership was erratic and contributed to Germany's eventual defeat; Hitler himself committed suicide in his bunker in Berlin in the last days of the war.

Hope, Bob

U.S. entertainer. Comedian and singer Bob Hope was one of the biggest movie stars at the start of the war. He became famous for his constant tours of U.S. overseas bases to put on shows for service personnel. Having performed similar tours in later wars in Korea, Vietnam and the Persian Gulf, Hope was acknowledged in 1997 by the U.S. Congress as the first 'Honorary Veteran' in U.S. history.

MacArthur, Douglas

U.S. general. A veteran of World War I, MacArthur commanded the defence of the Philippines against Japan in 1941 before becoming supreme Allied commander in the Southwest Pacific. He commanded the U.S. attacks on New Guinea and the Philippines. After the end of the war, he became supreme Allied commander of Japan and oversaw the country's rapid postwar recovery.

Miller, Dorrie

Miller was an African-American seaman who served at Pearl Harbor in December 1941. Although at the time African Americans were only allowed to serve as orderlies, his courage during the Japanese attack earned him the Navy Cross and made him a national hero.

Montgomery, Bernard

British field marshal. Montgomery led the British Eighth Army in North Africa, where it defeated Rommel's Afrika Korps, and then shared joint command of the invasion of Sicily and Italy. He collaborated with U.S. general Eisenhower on planning the D-Day landings in France, where he commanded all land forces; Montgomery went on to command an army group in the advance toward Germany, where he eventually received the German surrender.

Mussolini, Benito

Italian dictator. Mussolini came to power in Italy in 1922 promoting fascism, a political philosophy based on a militaristic form of nationalism. He led attempts to re-create an Italian empire with overseas conquests. Mussolini became Hitler's ally in 1936 and entered the war on the Nazis' side. Italian campaigns went badly in the Balkans and North Africa, however. When the Allies invaded Italy in 1943 Mussolini was sacked by the king; he became president of a puppet German republic in northern Italy. He was executed by Italian partisan fighters at the end of the war.

Rommel, Erwin

German field marshal. Rommel was a tank commander who led the Afrika Korps in North Africa and later led the defence of northern France against the Allied invasion. When he was discovered to be part of a plot to assassinate Adolf Hitler, he was forced to commit suicide.

Roosevelt, Franklin D.

U.S. president. Democrat politician Franklin Delano Roosevelt enjoyed a privileged upbringing before entering politics and becoming governor of New York. He first came to power as president in 1932, when he was elected to apply his New Deal to solve the worst problems of the Great Depression. Reelected in 1936 and again in 1940 he fully supported the Allies, offering supplies to help fight the Germans. He was reelected in 1944, the only president to be elected for four terms, but died in office shortly before the end of the war against Japan.

Rosie the Riveter

A fictional American worker who first appeared in a popular song but whose image then appeared on posters and stamps to encourage women to take industrial jobs during the war. The various depictions of Rosie were based on a number of specific individual workers.

Stalin, Joseph

Soviet dictator. Stalin was a Bolshevik from Georgia who rose to prominence for his skill as an administrator. In 1922 he became general secretary of the Communist Party of the Soviet Union founded by Lenin. Stalin introduced programs to encourage agriculture and industry and in the 1930s got rid of many thousands of potential enemies in purges, having them jailed or executed. Having made a pact with Hitler in 1939, he was surprised when Hitler invaded the Soviet Union in 1941 but rallied the Red Army to eventual victory. At the end of the war, he imposed Soviet rule on eastern Europe.

Yamamoto, Isoroko

Japanese admiral. Yamamoto was a visionary naval planner who planned Japan's attack on the U.S. base at Pearl Harbor and its early Pacific campaigns. He was killed when the Americans shot down his aircraft in 1943, alerted by decoded Japanese radio communications.

Glossary

Allies One of the two groups of combatants in the war. The main Allies were Britain, the Soviet Union, the United States, British Empire troops, and free forces from occupied nations.

antibiotic A medicine that can halt the spread of infection.

anti-Semitism A hatred of Jews and Judaism.

armistice A temporary halt in fighting agreed to by both sides.

armour A term referring to armoured vehicles, such as tanks.

artillery Large weapons such as big guns and howitzers.

Aryan In Nazi propaganda, relating to a mythical master race of Nordic peoples.

Axis One of the two groups of combatants in the war. The leading Axis powers were Germany, Italy, and Japan.

blitzkrieg A German word meaning "lightning war." It referred to the tactic of rapid land advance supported by great airpower.

Bolsheviks Members of the Communist Party that took power in Russia after the 1917 Revolution.

casualty Someone who is killed or wounded in conflict, or who is missing but probably dead.

collaborator Someone who works with members of enemy forces who are occupying his or her country.

communism A political philosophy based on state control of the economy and distribution of wealth, followed in the Soviet Union from 1917 and in China from 1948.

corps A military formation smaller than an army, made up of a number of divisions operating together under a general.

counteroffensive A set of attacks that defend against enemy attacks.

empire A number of countries governed by a single country.

embargo An order to temporarily stop something, especially trading.

espionage The use of spies or secret agents to obtain information about the plans of a foreign government.

evacuation The act of moving someone from danger to a safe position.

Fascism A political philosophy promoted by Mussolini in Italy based on dictatorial leadership, nationalism and the importance of the state over the individual.

garrison A group of troops placed to defend a location.

Holocaust The systematic German campaign to exterminate millions of Jews and others.

hygiene Following practices, such as keeping clean, that support the maintenance of good health.

independence The state of self-government for a people or nation.

infantry Soldiers who are trained to fight on foot, or in vehicles.

kamikaze Japanese for "divine wind"; the name refers to Japan's suicide pilots.

landing craft Shallow-bottomed boats designed to carry troops and supplies from ships to the shore.

Marine A soldier who serves in close association with naval forces.

materiel A word that describes all the equipment and supplies used by military forces.

morale A sense of common purpose and positive spirits among a group of people or a whole population

occupation The seizure and control of an area by military force.

offensive A planned military attack.

patriotism A love for and promotion of one's country.

propaganda Material such as images, broadcasts or writings that aims to influence the ideas or behaviour of a group of people.

rationing A system of limiting food and other supplies to ensure that everyone gets a similar amount.

reconnaissance A small-scale survey of enemy territory to gather information.

resources Natural materials that are the basis of economic wealth, such as oil, rubber, and agricultural produce.

strategy A detailed plan for achieving success.

strongpoint Any defensive position that has been strengthened to withstand an attack.

siege A military blockade of a place, such as a city, to force it to surrender.

taxes Fees on earnings or financial transactions used by governments to raise money from their citizens.

troops Groups of soldiers.

war bonds A form of investment used by governments in wartime to raise money from savers.

Further Reading

Books

Adams, Simon. *Occupation and Resistance* (Documenting World War II). Wayland, 2008.

Black, Hermann. *World War II, 1939–1945* (Wars Day-by-Day). Brown Bear Reference, 2008.

The Blitz. World War II Replica Memorabilia Pack. Resources for Teaching, 2010.

Burgan, Michael. *America in World War II* (Wars That Changed American History). World Almanac Library, 2006.

Cross, Vince. *Blitz: a Wartime Girl's Diary, 1940–1941* (My Story). Scholastic, 2008.

Deary, Terry, and Mike Phillips. *The Blitz* (Horrible Histories Handbooks). Scholastic 2009.

Dowswell, Paul. *Usborne Introduction to the Second World War.* Usborne Publishing Ltd., 2005.

Gardiner, Juliet. *The Children's War: The Second World War Through the Eyes of the Children of Britain.* Portrait, 2005.

Heppelwhite, Peter. *An Evacuee's Journey* (History Journeys). Wayland, 2004.

Hosch, William L. *World War II: People, Politics and Power* (America at War). Rosen Education Service, 2009.

MacDonald, Fiona. *World War II: Life on the Home Front: A Primary Source History* (In Their Own Words). Gareth Stevens Publishing, 2009.

McNeese, Tim. *World War II: 1939–1945* (Discovering U.S. History). Chelsea House Publishers, 2010.

O'Shei, Tim. *World War II Spies.* Edge Books, 2008.

Price, Sean. *Rosie the Riveter: Women in World War II.* Raintree, 2008.

Price, Sean. *The Art of War: The Posters of World War II* (American History Through Primary Sources). Raintree, 2008.

Ross, Stuart. *The Blitz* (At Home in World War II). Evans Brothers, 2007.

Ross, Stuart. *Evacuation* (At Home in World War II). Evans Brothers, 2007.

Ross, Stuart. *Rationing* (At Home in World War II). Evans Brothers, 2007.

Tonge, Neil. *The Rise of the Nazis* (Documentary World War II). Wayland, 2008.

Wagner, Melissa, and Dan Bryant. *The Big Book of World War II: Fascinating Facts about World War II Including Maps, Historic Photographs and Timelines.* Perseus Books, 2009.

World War II (10 volumes). Grolier Educational, 2006.

World War II (Eyewitness). Dorling Kindersley, 2007.

Websites

www.bbc.co.uk/history/worldwars/wwtwo/
Causes, events and people of the war.

http://www.bbc.co.uk/schools/primaryhistory/world_war2/
Interactive information on what it was like to be a child during the war.

http://www.spartacus.schoolnet.co.uk/2WW.htm
Spartacus Education site on the war.

http://www.nationalarchives.gov.uk/education/worldwar2/
U.S. National Archives primary sources on the war.

http://www.historylearningsite.co.uk/WORLD%20WAR%20TWO.htm
History Learning Site guide to the war.

http://www.telegraph.co.uk/news/newstopics/world-war-2/
Daily Telegraph archive of articles from wartime and from the 70th anniversary of its outbreak.

www.war-experience.org
The Second World War Experience Centre.

www.ibiblio.org/pha
A collection of primary World War II source materials.

www.worldwar-2.net
Complete World War II day-by-day timeline.

http://www.iwm.org.uk/searchlight/server.php?change=SearchlightGalleryView&changeNav=home
Imperial War Museum, London, guide to collections.

Index